Monthly Limericks

A Limerick Collection for Every Month

by
Just Limericks

Table of Contents

Get ready to laugh and be entertained with these classic style limericks! Each limerick is a cleverly crafted masterpiece of wordplay and wit, sure to leave you with a smile on your face. With classic style limericks for every month of the year, you'll never run out of charming and humorous rhymes to enjoy.

From the icy chill of January to the lazy days of August and the festive spirit of December, each month has its own unique character and inspiration for these limericks. These whimsical and playful verses are known for their light-hearted and humorous tone, featuring unexpected twists and turns that will have you chuckling in delight.

Whether you're in the mood for a clever pun or a silly rhyme, these classic style limericks are sure to bring some fun and joy to your day. So sit back, relax, and let the limericks do the talking – you're in for a treat!

January

In January, the air is cold,

But the heart can be warm and bold,

With the snow on the ground,

And the icicles all around,

It's a time to cherish and hold.

Oh, January, so dark and cold,

Yet the world is still full of gold,

With fires in the hearth,

And love in the heart,

It's a time to be brave and bold.

In January, the nights are long,

But the stars in the sky are strong,

With the moon up high,

And the snowdrifts nigh,

It's a time for a cozy song.

January can be dreary,

But the heart can still be cheery,

With friends by the fire,

And hot cocoa to inspire,

It's a time to be warm and merry.

In January, the snow may fall,

And the winds may howl and call,

But inside it's warm,

With no cause for alarm,

It's a time to embrace it all.

Oh, January, with its icy chill,

But the heart can be warmer still,

With love all around,

And joy to be found,

It's a time to savor and thrill.

January may be bleak,

But the future is still to seek,

With hopes and dreams,

And plans and schemes,

It's a time to be strong and meek.

In January, the world is new,

And there's so much to explore and do,

With snowmen to make,

And memories to take,

It's a time to be happy and true.

Oh, January, so quiet and still,
But there's life in the air to fill,
With laughter and love,
And warmth from above,
It's a time to take in the thrill.

In January, the world is white,
And the days can be long and bright,
With a snowball to throw,
And love to bestow,
It's a time to cherish the light.

February

February, the month of love,

With hearts and flowers up above,

With Cupid's bow,

And kisses aglow,

It's a time for romance to shove.

Oh, February, so cold and clear,

But the heart can still hold so dear,

With hot chocolate and hugs,

And cozy snug rugs,

It's a time to be happy and near.

In February, the days grow long,

And the nights are full of song,

With love in the air,

And hearts to share,

It's a time to be brave and strong.

February, with its snow and ice,

But there's warmth in the heart so nice,

With friends by the fire,

And family to inspire,

It's a time to be merry and wise.

In February, the world turns red,

With love in every word that's said,

With hearts to fill,

And dreams to spill,

It's a time to be fearless and led.

Oh, February, with its magic spell,

And its tales of love to tell,

With roses in bloom,

And hearts to consume,

It's a time to be under love's spell.

February, with its winter breeze,

And its moments that time will freeze,

With memories to keep,

And promises to leap,

It's a time to be loved and please.

In February, the love abounds,

With hearts that are true and profound,

With smiles that shine,

And love to entwine,

It's a time to be lost and found.

Oh, February, with its mystery,

And its tales of love and history,

With hearts to win,

And souls to spin,

It's a time to be happy and free.

In February, the love will soar,

With hearts that are full and more,

With passion and fire,

And dreams that inspire,

It's a time to be loved to the core.

March

March comes in like a lion so wild,

With winds that blow like a tempest so styled,

With rains that pour,

And a chill to the core,

It's a time to be hearty and riled.

Oh, March, with its green so bright,

And the promise of spring in sight,

With buds to bloom,

And skies to consume,

It's a time to be full of delight.

In March, the days grow longer,

And the birds sing a sweeter song,

With the sun's warm rays,

And spring's lovely ways,

It's a time to be happy and strong.

March brings a madness to the air,

With college hoops and brackets to share,

With Cinderella teams,

And the Final Four dreams,

It's a time to cheer and declare.

Oh, March, with its Irish pride,

And the shamrocks to be spied,

With the leprechauns' gold,

And stories so bold,

It's a time to be happy inside.

In March, the world begins anew,

With life and growth in view,

With gardens to tend,

And seeds to befriend,

It's a time to start fresh and true.

March, with its windy ways,

And its bluster that makes us sway,

With kites to fly,

And windsurfing to try,

It's a time to be wild and gay.

Oh, March, with its lion and lamb,

And the changes that come with a cram,

With winter's last gasp,

And spring's sweet grasp,

It's a time to be brave and slam.

In March, the luck of the Irish,

With green beer and corned beef so delish,

With parades so grand,

And good cheer at hand,

It's a time to be happy and stylish.

March, with its madness and mirth,

And the joy that springs forth on the earth,

With laughter and glee,

And a sense of being free,

It's a time to enjoy life for all it's worth.

April

April showers bring May flowers, they say,

But the rain in April is here to stay,

With puddles to jump,

And umbrellas to hump,

It's a time to enjoy the wet spray.

Oh, April, with your Easter eggs bright,

And the pastel colors in our sight,

With bunnies so cute,

And chocolate to suit,

It's a time to savor with delight.

In April, the world awakens anew,

With the blossoms and buds in view,

With trees in bloom,

And nature's perfume,

It's a time to be happy and true.

April is the time of rebirth,

With nature's cycle here on Earth,

With birds that sing,

And the promise of spring,

It's a time to renew our worth.

Oh, April, with your tax day in sight,

And the deadline that causes a fright,

With forms to fill,

And a bill to fulfill,

It's a time to be wise and contrite.

In April, the baseball season begins,

With games and players and all their grins,

With hot dogs and beer,

And the crack of the bat so clear,

It's a time to enjoy the wins.

April, with your Earth Day so green,

And the focus on nature's scene,

With recycling and reuse,

And sustainable news,

It's a time to care for what's been.

Oh, April, with your April Fool's Day,

And the pranks that come out to play,

With jokes so sly,

And laughter so high,

It's a time to enjoy the display.

In April, the spring break is near,

With students and teachers all in good cheer,

With trips to take,

And memories to make,

It's a time to let go of the year.

April, with your cherry blossoms so fair,

And the beauty that's everywhere,

With gardens to tend,

And the world to befriend,

It's a time to enjoy life and care.

May

In the merry month of May,

The flowers bloomed in bright array,

The birds sang sweetly,

As the days passed fleetly,

And the sun shone on day by day.

In May, the weather is fine,

With clear skies and warm sunshine,

The trees are in bloom,

And there's no sense of gloom,

It's a time for joy and good wine.

Oh, the month of May is so fair,

With its sunshine and warm summer air,

The meadows are green,

And the sky is serene,

It's a time to forget all our care.

In May, the world is alive,

And all around, the bees hive,

The flowers are in bloom,

And there's no sense of gloom,

It's a time to be happy and thrive.

In the month of May, so bright,

The sun shines with all its might,

The days are long,

And the birds sing their song,

It's a time to feel alive and light.

Oh, the month of May, how sublime,

With its warm and gentle clime,

The sky is blue,

And the grass is too,

It's a time to relax and unwind.

May brings the sweet scent of flowers,

And the gentle springtime showers,

The world is reborn,

On this day we were sworn,

To enjoy the world's beautiful powers.

The month of May is a delight,

With its colors, so bold and bright,

The world comes alive,

As the bees and birds thrive,

It's a time of joy and pure light.

In May, the world is so green,

With new life in every scene,

The sun is so bright,

And the air is so light,

It's a time to be happy and keen.

Oh, the month of May, how grand,

With its sun and its warm, gentle hand,

The world is at peace,

And all troubles cease,

It's a time to enjoy the beautiful land.

June

Oh, June, with your sun shining bright,

And the warmth that brings such delight,

With pools to cool off,

And ice cream to scoff,

It's a time to bask in the light.

In June, the school year comes to an end,

With diplomas and caps to defend,

With parties to throw,

And goodbyes to know,

It's a time to celebrate and blend.

June is the month for weddings so fine,

With dresses and suits and a long line,

With vows to exchange,

And rings to arrange,

It's a time for love to intertwine.

In June, the days are long and hot,

With picnics and BBQs in the spot,

With burgers and fries,

And lemonade to prize,

It's a time to gather and trot.

Oh, June, with your Father's Day near,

And the chance to show love without fear,

With cards to send,

And gifts to extend,

It's a time to show thanks and cheer.

June is the start of summer so sweet,

With vacations and trips to greet,

With sandy beaches,

And seashells to reaches,

It's a time to have fun in the heat.

In June, the flowers are in bloom,

With petals and colors to consume,

With gardens to tend,

And beauty to blend,

It's a time to enjoy nature's plume.

June, with your graduations galore,

And the hats that we toss in the air,

With speeches so wise,

And tears in our eyes,

It's a time to look forward and dare.

In June, the fireflies light up the night,

With magic and wonder in sight,

With lanterns to hold,

And stories to be told,

It's a time to experience delight.

June, with your Summer Solstice so grand,

And the longest day at our command,

With festivals to attend,

And traditions to extend,

It's a time to celebrate the land.

July

Oh, July, with your fireworks display,
And the colors that light up the way,
With sparklers to hold,
And stories to be told,
It's a time to enjoy the array.

In July, the beaches are alive,
With waves and sand and sun to thrive,
With cool waters to swim,
And towels to dry skin,
It's a time to take a dive.

July is the month of Independence Day,

With parades and picnics on the way,

With flags to wave,

And speeches to save,

It's a time to honor the USA.

Oh, July, with your hot summer days,

And the ice cream that cools in many ways,

With cones to lick,

And flavors to pick,

It's a time to savor the blaze.

In July, the gardens are in bloom,

With petals and colors to consume,

With bees to buzz,

And butterflies to fuss,

It's a time to smell the perfume.

July is the month of family vacations,

With memories to make in destinations,

With road trips to take,

And new adventures to make,

It's a time of fun explorations.

Oh, July, with your baseball games,

And the fans that cheer with such aims,

With balls to catch,

And bats to dispatch,

It's a time to play with no shames.

In July, the lakes and rivers are inviting,

With boats and canoes for exciting,

With fishing to do,

And paddleboarding too,

It's a time to enjoy the water's lighting.

July is the month of lazy afternoons,

With hammocks to swing to many tunes,

With books to read,

And naps to lead,

It's a time to relax until the moon.

Oh, July, with your warm summer nights,

And the stars that twinkle with such sights,

With campfires to light,

And s'mores to delight,

It's a time to enjoy the summer delights.

August

Oh, August, with your long summer days,

And the sun that shines in many ways,

With heat to bear,

And shades to wear,

It's a time to enjoy the rays.

In August, the beaches are still hot,

With sand and surf and waves to plot,

With sunsets to see,

And shells to be,

It's a time to enjoy the beach lot.

August is the month of picnics and fairs,

With cotton candy and games and chairs,

With pies to bake,

And lemonade to make,

It's a time for sweet summer airs.

Oh, August, with your garden harvest,

And the fruits and veggies to invest,

With corn to shuck,

And berries to pluck,

It's a time to enjoy what's best.

In August, the forests are alive,

With trails and hikes and views to thrive,

With birds to watch,

And wildlife to catch,

It's a time to be outdoor-wise.

August is the month of back-to-school,

With pencils and books and learning rule,

With teachers to meet,

And schedules to beat,

It's a time to be ready and cool.

Oh, August, with your meteor shower,

And the shooting stars that hold power,

With wishes to make,

And dreams to take,

It's a time to watch the cosmic tower.

In August, the nights are still warm,

With fireflies and crickets to charm,

With stargazing to do,

And memories to pursue,

It's a time to enjoy the night's form.

August is the month of new adventures,

With trips and travels and culture features,

With maps to read,

And landmarks to heed,

It's a time to explore without pressures.

Oh, August, with your last summer days,

And the memories that linger and stay,

With friends to hug,

And love to snug,

It's a time to enjoy the final rays.

September

Oh, September, with your autumn breeze,

And the leaves that fall from the trees,

With apples to pick,

And pies to lick,

It's a time to enjoy the cool ease.

In September, the gardens are bright,

With flowers and herbs and veggies in sight,

With pumpkins to grow,

And scarecrows to show,

It's a time to enjoy the harvest right.

September is the month of new beginnings,
With school and work and fresh winnings,
With pencils to sharpen,
And goals to harden,
It's a time to start fresh with new innings.

Oh, September, with your cooler nights,
And the stars that shine with new sights,
With bonfires to light,
And stories to recite,
It's a time to enjoy the autumn delights.

In September, the forests are ablaze,

With colors and hues in endless ways,

With trails to hike,

And wildlife to spike,

It's a time to enjoy the fall phase.

September is the month of change,

With weather and life rearrange,

With clothes to swap,

And routines to stop,

It's a time to adjust and rearrange.

Oh, September, with your full moon bright,

And the harvest that comes with its light,

With crops to store,

And traditions to explore,

It's a time to celebrate the autumn right.

In September, the skies are clear,

With birds and butterflies in the atmosphere,

With migration to watch,

And nature to catch,

It's a time to enjoy the outdoors without fear.

September is the month of reflection,

With memories and thoughts in recollection,

With gratitude to give,

And thanks to receive,

It's a time to appreciate life's perfection.

Oh, September, with your final days,

And the memories that time always saves,

With friends to cherish,

And love to nourish,

It's a time to enjoy the autumn blaze.

October

Oh, October, with your crisp air,

And the leaves that fall everywhere,

With pumpkins to carve,

And ghosts to starve,

It's a time to enjoy the fall's flair.

In October, the colors are bright,

With orange, yellow, and red in sight,

With apples to pick,

And cider to lick,

It's a time to savor the autumnal light.

October is the month of spooky,

With witches, goblins, and monsters kooky,

With costumes to wear,

And candy to share,

It's a time to get your scare on, rookie.

Oh, October, with your full moon,

And the stories that go with its tune,

With werewolves to howl,

And owls to prowl,

It's a time to enjoy the mystical boon.

In October, the nights are long,

With stars and constellations strong,

With bonfires to light,

And tales to recite,

It's a time to sing the autumn's song.

October is the month of harvest,

With fields of plenty and abundance that's vast,

With feasts to prepare,

And families to share,

It's a time to give thanks and be steadfast.

Oh, October, with your chilly breeze,

And the smell of cider and pumpkin spice that
please,

With hayrides to take,

And memories to make,

It's a time to embrace the autumn's tease.

In October, the forests are alive,

With creatures that scurry and thrive,

With hikes to take,

And nature to make,

It's a time to explore and strive.

October is the month of change,

With weather and life that rearrange,

With leaves to rake,

And routines to remake,

It's a time to embrace the new range.

Oh, October, with your final days,

And the memories that time always saves,

With love to give,

And life to live,

It's a time to enjoy the autumn's blaze.

November

Oh, November, with your crisp air,
And the scent of cinnamon everywhere,
With leaves that fall,
And turkeys that call,
It's a time to gather and share.

In November, the colors are rich,
With oranges, yellows, and browns that stitch,
With harvest to reap,
And memories to keep,
It's a time to enjoy the autumn's niche.

November is the month of gratitude,

With blessings to count and attitude,

With feasts to prepare,

And thanks to share,

It's a time to cherish the good and fortitude.

Oh, November, with your shorter days,

And the chill that creeps in every way,

With warm fires to light,

And cozy blankets to sight,

It's a time to embrace the comfort and stay.

In November, the skies are clear,

With stars that twinkle and appear,

With brisk walks to take,

And hot cocoa to make,

It's a time to enjoy the autumn's atmosphere.

November is the month of family,

With love that binds and camaraderie,

With stories to tell,

And memories to dwell,

It's a time to strengthen the bonds that carry.

Oh, November, with your bare trees,

And the sound of leaves that rustle with ease,

With pies to bake,

And love to make,

It's a time to enjoy the simple and seize.

In November, the world slows down,

With peace and quiet that abound,

With books to read,

And naps to need,

It's a time to relax and rebound.

November is the month of hope,

With new beginnings and ways to cope,

With goals to set,

And dreams to get,

It's a time to reach for the stars and elope.

Oh, November, with your final days,

And the memories that time always saves,

With thanks to give,

And life to live,

It's a time to enjoy the autumn's blaze.

December

In December, the air is cold,

And the ground is often covered with mold,

With snowmen to build,

And eggnog to swill,

It's a time to have fun, so be bold.

Oh, December, with your twinkling lights,

And the magic that comes with winter nights,

With carols to sing,

And gifts to bring,

It's a time to spread joy and delight.

In December, the season is bright,

With stars that shine and hearts that ignite,

With friends to meet,

And family to greet,

It's a time to love and unite.

December is the month of giving,

With generosity and gratitude living,

With stockings to stuff,

And cookies to fluff,

It's a time to cherish the act of forgiving.

Oh, December, with your cozy fires,

And the warmth that everyone admires,

With scarves to knit,

And mittens to fit,

It's a time to indulge in all that inspires.

In December, the days are short,

With time for reflection and resort,

With candles to light,

And memories in sight,

It's a time to appreciate and exhort.

December is the month of cheer,

With laughter and smiles that endear,

With trees to trim,

And songs to hymn,

It's a time to spread joy far and near.

Oh, December, with your frosty breath,

And the joy that comes with the festive wreath,

With sleigh bells to ring,

And snowflakes to fling,

It's a time to enjoy the season with zest.

In December, the nights are long,

With tales to tell and a lovely song,

With hot cocoa to sip,

And presents to unwrap,

It's a time to make memories that are strong.

December is the month of magic,

With wonder and awe that are tragic,

With snow to play,

And love to convey,

It's a time to believe in miracles and fantastic.

www.justlimericks.com